Walk With Me
Into The Light

SOME COMFORT ON THE JOURNEY THROUGH GRIEF

First published in 2015 by Messenger Publications

ISBN 9781910248133

Designed by Messenger Publications Design Department
Typeset in Centaur and SF Scribbled Sans
Printed by Naas Printing Ltd

MESSENGER
PUBLICATIONS
JESUITS in IRELAND

Messenger Publications,
37 Lower Leeson Street, Dublin 2
www.messenger.ie

Introduction

In life we all experience many ups and downs. We can have moments of great joy but simultaneously interspersed within the joy of life there can also be seconds, minutes, days of deep sorrow and pain.

The love of a spouse, the birth of a child, the much sought after promotion at work or the holiday of a lifetime can all bring a smile to our face that radiates our heart and our soul. Life can be so good, so full of happiness and love. Life can be exhilarating. Our world can at times be so full of light, hope and potential – we feel as if we can do anything or that we can truly be the person we want to be. There is nothing that can put an end to the array of possibilities that now seem to be ahead of us. We are strong, and have time and energy on our side. As Saint Paul assures us in Romans 8:31, 'With God on our side who could be against us?' Walking the pathway of life with God on our side can be so fulfilling, so full of love and happiness.

But, sadly, life is not always filled with moments that we will remember fondly and with affection. There are times when clouds instead of sunshine begin to inhabit our horizons. We can find ourselves challenged to carry heavy burdens and oftentimes we can feel very lost and alone. The joy that the world promises is no longer ours. The spark within has quenched. We can become frozen in a second of pain that never leaves us. Life can be so very unpredictable – changing forever in the blink of an eye. We can find ourselves thrown into a situation we never dreamed we would have to face, where all that was certain and secure is no more. Without warning, we can find the parameters of our lives redrawn – our smile turned to a tear. The heart that was once so light, replaced by one weighed down heavily by a rock of pain. Loss has invaded our lives and shattered the equilibrium that once was ours.

In life, our losses come in many different shapes and sizes, but whatever they are they affect us deeply. We can feel bereft and disappointed when we lose our job, fail an exam or when we have our loan application turned down. We can feel hurt when a relationship ends or when the much longed for baby is not to be. We feel betrayed when our loyalty has not been repaid or when our trusted confidant has let us down. We can feel pained when life simply has not turned out the way we had hoped it would. Shattered dreams, broken promises or the feeling of being alone in the world can all leave us heaving in pain – with our hopes replaced by overwhelming hopelessness – the light turned to darkness.

Perhaps the greatest cross we are asked to carry is the death of a loved one. Human beings are made to live in relationship and, intentionally or unintentionally, all our worlds are shaped and defined by those with whom we have formed a human connection. The loss of one we loved with all our heart and soul is the greatest of all pains to feel and to carry. When we lose a spouse, a partner, a parent, a child, a sibling, a neighbour or a friend we lose part of ourselves, because tied up in this person is part of our inner being. When we lose someone close to us, we have become changed forever, having lost part of what it is that makes us who we are. We may not realise it, but every human being who touches our heart forms part of us. Every human connection helps our heart and our soul to grow and the loss of their love is a pain so very hard to bear.

We lose people that we love in many different ways; through old age; infirmity; illness; miscarriage; stillbirth; suicide; accidents and whether suddenly or with warning their loss shatters our world. Nothing ever really prepares us for the finality of death. We can think and believe that we know what it will feel like but, in essence, we do not really know until death affects us personally how overwhelmingly final it is. It is the loss of human connection. It is the breaking of a bond that, in many cases, has existed for many, many years. Memories have been formed, experiences shared, plans made for the future and suddenly there will be no more. The love lives on but the physical presence is gone. Never will we touch or hear or see the person we once loved so very much.

Imagine how difficult it must be for a couple who have shared their whole adult lives together to now have their bond broken? People speak of feeling bereft, alone, unable to survive as one when they had been two for so long. Even when they have had the gift of a family, the loneliness and desolation can be overwhelming. The pain of having to start again, at having to walk through the world alone when they once had an ever-present companion by their side can be so frightening. It can take months, years indeed before a person feels strong enough to face living again.

Or there is the sibling who now stands alone, having lost all other members from their family of origin. They are now a stranger in a world that is very changed. There may not now be a family home to return to visit. They have found themselves alone, locked in a world of grief. Even when they have a family of their own, the loss of that familiar bond can be heart breaking. For the parent whose arms longed to hold a baby but now embrace emptiness, this is a gap that can never be filled. No words, no reassurances, no gestures will ever replace their shattered hopes and dreams. The loss of a loved one – be it baby, child or adult – is a cross so very heavy to carry. Although their memory lives on inside of us it can be so very difficult to accept that the person we love will no longer be a tangible part of our daily existence. Death is so cold, so final and so all consuming.

When we lose a loved one, we can be filled with a broad spectrum of emotions. Indeed the normal response to loss is grief. The length and depth of our grief is dependent very much upon the nature of the attachment to the person we have lost or are about to lose. Often we feel like we have never done before, and as though no one could ever possibly understand the pain that now inhabits our heart and our soul. We have been catapulted into a place that we do not fit into, and yet we know not how to come out of it. Even when we are in company, we can feel disconnected and alone. Even when there are voices and words spoken all we hear is the silence – the silence of our pain. This world has become a stranger to us. We feel as if we no longer belong here. No one can see, hear or feel our pain. No one can see the tears fighting to be contained within one whose heart has been broken. We can feel misunderstood and disconnected from reality. We are told by well-intentioned friends and family members that we need to pull ourselves together and get on with our lives. We are counselled that we ought to be grateful for the love that we have shared and experienced and the memories that we have. We are told what we should do and how we should feel. Well-meaning family members and friends try to help us move on, but their lives move on while we struggle to shoulder the weight of our grief. Their probing and their words can prove so very infuriating as we do not want to be told how to feel, how to act, or how to survive this horrible moment in our lives.

These are harsh words and yet such empty ones. Wouldn't I get on with things if only I could? Wouldn't I make sense of it all if I could? Wouldn't I breathe a sigh of relief if my aching heart allowed it? Death locks us into a world of pain and isolation. In this world of pain we become untouchable, and are unable to move on. The loss of our loved one is a mountain too high to climb, a river too deep to swim and the failure of others to touch our pain or sit with it can make us feel like an oddity. Sometimes we can feel as if we would be better off to retreat into a world of safety forever where we will be left alone, untouched by the discomfort of the outside world, a world not able to hold our pain, a world that fears to speak of death. People want us to move on as to speak of death causes a certain degree of discomfort. If we are alright, then we won't speak of death or pain or loss. Our pain taps into a world that people do not want to imagine or want to try to understand. Our pain unnerves others. It threatens to dismantle their world of equilibrium and balance. Our pain challenges others to explore how they feel about death.

Where is God in all of this? Is there a God at all, people often ask in the aftermath of a death. At times of loss and especially after we lose a loved one, we can feel totally and utterly abandoned by our God. Suddenly it can feel like there is no God. We can feel disconnected from God. Harsh words can be spoken to God as we can sense that He has let us down. 'How could God let this happen to me?' many ask as their hearts ache in pain. How is it that after all my attempts to do the right thing, this is how I have been repaid? The cries of the psalmist in psalm 73 echos within when we feel that prosperity and reward is preserved only for the wicked and for us only judgement, heartache and pain. We can feel that He has become a cold and distant entity. The image of the Good Shepherd, put before us in Matthew 18 and Luke 15 who sought out his lost and lonely sheep, has begun to feel false and meaningless. He no longer inhabits our world it would seem. He has become disconnected from our pain. In our pain and experience of death we can become alienated from the all-loving and compassionate God that we have heard about so many times. We feel as though God is no longer part of our picture, and our world is devoid of a God who cares.

Theology or words of reassurance can feel cold and empty – meaningless expressions of sorrow. When we have lost a loved one our prayers can dry up. We can no longer find it in our hearts to speak to the God who is seen to have taken our loved one from us. In the aftermath of a loss or life changing experience, people often speak of not having the energy to pray. The inclination to place the worries of our heart at the foot of the Cross has disappeared. Our words fail us because we feel that God has let us down. We feel disappointed. We feel totally and utterly alone. There is no heart in our prayers so hence they have no meaning. Even those who have prayed religiously for years can at times like this, now have no energy left to entreat a God they once loved so deeply and so unquestionably, for help. Why pray when the answers will not come, when the gravity of our situation cannot be changed? Even in the silence words cannot be found. There is no space to pray. No words will come to us in our darkness.

But for others, it is only their prayers, their connection with God, their link with their protector God that can and will sustain them in the desolation of their pain. For some prayer is the only thing that can help them to travel the roadway of loss and grief. Understanding may evade but the hope in a God who holds all of us in the palm of his hand is all that can support and sustain at this point. Only God the Father can truly feel the pain of one who has lost their loved one. Imagine the pain of Mary as she stood at the foot of the Cross (John 19: 25) and looked up at the child she carried within her womb for nine months. Imagine the deep, deep sorrow she must have felt as she heard her beloved son cry out in pain and desolation. Imagine how her soul must have heaved in pain as she watched her son Jesus being battered and bruised on the Cross. Only God knew the pain that permeated her heart, soul and mind on that Good Friday evening.

Death hits each and every one of us very hard. Having said that, it is the one thing we all have a reluctance to speak about. Yet, it is the one sure thing that we will all have to face, both personally and communally. There is no avoiding death. Where there is life there is the potential for death and pain and loss. But we all vary in how we react to death. As we are all different in the foods we eat, the music we listen to or the books that we read, so too are we unique in how we react to death.

Indeed, there really is no way to anticipate how we will react to the death of a loved one until we have to face it. Neither is there a blueprint to follow that tells us how we 'should' or 'must' react when we are bereaved. Nor is there any sort of roadmap, which guides us through our grief. The reality is that the heavy weight of grief is carried the way that best suits each of us. We do it the best way that we can.

There is no right way or wrong way to grieve. We all do it the only way we know how. We stumble and fall and we struggle for survival amid a whirlwind of pain, loss and grief. When our world is shattered into millions of tiny pieces the only way to put together a broken heart and soul is to do it slowly and with compassion, patience and love.

However, this booklet is an attempt to walk the journey of loneliness with the person whose heart has been broken by the loss of their beloved. As Jesus walked side by side on the road to Emmaus with his disciples (Luke 24: 13-25) whose hearts were broken, this little book is a companion on your journey of pain and loss. Take this book within your hands and carry it with you as you travel the roadway of life. As you attempt to re-define your world in the wake of your loss, use it as your companion on the road to a new beginning, not forgetting but remembering with love, and to living with a smile in your heart for those who are now gone home to God.

If someone close to you is experiencing the pain of loss, use this book as a guide to how best to accompany him or her and support them on their new journey, walking with them through the darkness to the light of a new beginning.

In 1969, Elisabeth Kubler Ross in her book *On Death and Dying* outlined what she termed the five stages of grief – denial, anger, bargaining, depression and acceptance. These were initially devised by Kubler Ross to describe the array of emotions and feelings which people facing death would journey through. However, these are now commonly accepted as the stages of grief which are experienced by people facing their own death or that of a loved one as well as endured by those who are grieving other significant losses in their lives. There are many other theories that can be applied to grief, loss and bereavement – such as one developed by Bowlby in 1969 or Parkes in 1971 – but it is Kubler Ross's model I will draw on here. These five stages as constructed by her will provide the framework for this little booklet. Whether the grief is anticipatory or experienced in the here and now, it is important to say that we all walk through the stages differently and possibly several times and certainly not in the same sequence as another person does. In essence, there is no definitive way to grieve. We all do it the best way that we know how. By feeling the emotions associated with the loss, we do our very best to journey towards a time, a day or a moment when we are strong enough to walk with courage and hope once more. We strive, often without having the ability to articulate it, to be able to accept and adjust to the new reality, which is now ours.

Denial: a survival tactic?

When we are faced with the death of a loved one our reaction can be somewhat surreal. We can find ourselves locked in a world of disbelief. We can become numb to the reality of what is unfolding around us. There is a sort of suspension of disbelief. If we don't feel it then it isn't real. If we do not allow ourselves to talk about the loss then maybe it did not happen after all. Many times it can be weeks, months or even years before a person is ready to accept the loss of a loved one. The loss is so raw and cuts so deeply that it simply cannot be spoken of or processed. This can be particularly true for a woman who has carried a baby within her womb for weeks or months only to lose it through late miscarriage or stillbirth. Or for a person who has been bereaved by suicide. Or for those who have lost a loved one as a result of a car accident. The gravity of the situation is too painful to face so denial protects the inner equilibrium. Walls are built around the heart of one whose heart has been broken. Blocking out the pain of the loss carves some distance from the harsh, painful world that has now become the new reality. Denial becomes the building blocks of the world of one who now needs self-preservation. The fear of crumbling can be too heavy a burden to carry so the tool of denial kicks in. This stage of grief can make us untouchable and unreachable. We begin to inhabit the world of the fortress. We become locked away from the painful reality of our new life.

While in this stage of grief, a person can move seemingly unaffected by the tragic loss they have just experienced. In fact, one can appear so unmoved by the death that those around them can feel as if they have been untouched by the death of their loved one. Indeed, family members can become angry towards the person who appears untouched or unmoved by the death of their loved one. There can be a feeling of disbelief by our family and friends at what looks like our tendency to be cold and aloof when we have suddenly become the bereaved person. We can be viewed as cold, icicles of immovable emotion when sadly the polar opposite is the reality. The disbelief shields us from the 'immediate' pain of our loss.

Oftentimes, people simply get on with it, returning to work or other activities as if nothing had happened. There is an attempt to simply get on with life, back to normal, just like we were. Work, studies or travel can make the world seem more bearable. Any distraction that will create a distance from reality becomes much sought after. If I cannot be touched by my loss then it will not be real. Denial has become the only survival tool that I know. It is the only thing that preserves sanity so I embrace it tightly, fearful of letting go. Opening my broken heart to the reality of my loss is simply not an option.

This can be an extremely lonely and frustrating time for family members. When for example, a wife loses her husband, she can unintentionally block out her children. She cannot handle her own pain and so by extension, cannot hold or acknowledge their pain either. She can alienate them so that they can feel a second loss. They have lost their father and now, through his death, have also lost their mother too. A chasm can open up because she is unable to relate to the world of their grief as a consequence of her denial of her own loss. Adult children can carry years of resentment towards their surviving parent when they have been disconnected from them in the aftermath of the family's deep loss. There can be layers of anger, resentment, bitterness, pain and desolation when grief becomes intertwined in family relationships. So much pain, such desolation, such desperation when one becomes disconnected from family members and friends in the aftermath of the death of a loved one.

It can also be very hurtful for family members and friends who try to reach out to the person mourning, who is unable to respond to their love and concern. In the creation of a world of disbelief, the person who is bereaved has ensured that no one will penetrate his or her pain. They can feel like their love and concern has been thrown back in their faces, unappreciated and unwanted. It is at times like this when friends and relatives can feel locked out, unloved and in some way to blame for the inability of the bereaved person to connect with them or to speak with them. In the quest to support our friend, or neighbour or our relative we have been disempowered. Denial has become a wall between us. No one can penetrate the rock that is now carried within the heart and the soul of one whose world has been shattered.

Where is God in all of this?

At this stage, God sits where He always does. In crafting a world of make-believe, a detachment from reality, the God of my every day still exists. Even when we feel that he is not there, God is there with us walking the journey of brokenness with us. So whatever image of God we are drawn to is the one we now cling to. The hand of a suffering God is extended to the broken-hearted even when they know not how to carry their pain. Blessed are those who mourn, for they shall be comforted (Matthew 5:4).

What am I to do?

The Bereaved

In the rawness of grief there is a tendency just to block out the pain. There are days when all I want to do is run while other days all I wish to do is pretend it never happened. In order to maintain my sanity I just need to keep going, come what may. Each day, do just as you are able to do. If you wish to be alone then be alone. If you want to be in company, seek out the friend who understands you the most and who is willing and able to hear your pain. Cry if you feel able and if not, just simply be. Sit and stay in the moment of disbelief. This is as far as you can take your pain for now.

The Companion on the Journey

In the frustration of disconnection, there can be a tendency to run away and let the bereaved person to his or her own devices. But instead try to stay with them where they are at. Try not to judge them and even when your advances are not appreciated, continue to reach out with love, empathy and compassion. The ability to sit with the pain of another is not easy but by so doing you are personifying the love of a God who loves each of us as we are.

Anger:
the walls of the
Fortress begin to crumble

This is the stage of grief that sees the dismantling of the walls of protection that have preserved a person through the earlier moments of grief. The reality is beginning to dawn that our beloved is gone forever. The enormity of the loss is now becoming so very evident. Never again will we hear their voice, feel their touch or drown in their laughter. The little things that we loved about them will never again touch us.

For many people, their anger can become quite acute when they have passed a milestone occasion such as a birthday or an anniversary. For others, anger can become aroused when a number of years have passed by. The reality is that they are never coming back to us. Their loss is final and there is no coming back from his painful realisation. The vacuum left by our loved one's passing is filled with anger, such deep-seated anger.

The fortress that we built to protect ourselves earlier has collapsed, and once more our parameters have been redrawn. Our world has been re-created and no longer is it inhabited by a feeling of disbelief but rather by anger. Anger is such a strong emotion.

When we are angry nothing else matters. Anger can cloud judgment and can make us say and do things that we normally would not. Anger is a boulder that weighs us down. Anger can make us feel as if we are drowning or suffocating. But anger also hides our pain. Anger can mask the deep, deep hurt which we are realising inhabits our heart.

But who are we angry with? We can of course be angry with ourselves. We are annoyed and possibly guilty at feeling the way we do. We are overwhelmed by the anger that prevents us from living our lives the way we once did. We are angry with ourselves because we are feeling lost and alone. We are angry because our comprehension has become skewed. We are angry because we do not really understand how or why we are feeling the way we do. Our inability to get on with things the way we once did is frustrating us. We are so angry that we cannot just get on with our lives. We are angry because we really do not want to feel the way we do. We are angry because our anger disempowers us.

We are angry because we have lost our zest for life. We no longer want to go out and do things. We want to be alone. We want to be left to wallow and to feel the way we do without interference or dictating from those around us. People speak of screaming inside with the sheer weight of their pain. People speak of shouting loudly while no sound comes. The pain is so penetrating that it has rendered them speechless. Many people say that all they want to do is to be left alone to cry, to shout or to simply be as they are. Sometimes the bereaved simply want to be able to feel the rawness of their grief.

However, much of the anger at self can actually stem from anger with a world that cannot relate to their pain. In a world that celebrates strength, success, power and glory, there is a reticence to speak of that which is not positive. There is a degree of reluctance by people around us to really hear the soul pain of one who is grieving. Pain is hard to shoulder, tears difficult to see so the world wants us to get on with it. Oftentimes we are angry with a world that is afraid of death, afraid of facing the raw pain of those who simply want to be held and loved by those around them. We can become angry because there is no one there who is strong enough to touch our pain, to reach into our wounds, to help shoulder our cross like Simon of Cyrene did for Jesus (Mark 15:21).

We can also be angry with the person who has died. We can feel guilty about this, but the reality is that we can feel huge resentment and anger towards the person who we once loved and is now dead. Why did they have to die? Why did they have to leave me? Did they not love me enough to stay? Why didn't they have more treatment? Why couldn't they have looked after themselves a bit better? Anger with the deceased person can be crippling as it can feel somewhat irrational and undeserved. This type of anger is common if their loss was sudden – by suicide or accident perhaps. There is an anger connected to the feeling that they have blocked us out, that somehow in failing to speak of their pain to us – that they did not love us. The child once in my womb has rejected me, or the person I promised my life to in marriage has not trusted me enough to tell me of their soul pain. My beloved didn't love me enough to fight a little harder for survival.

There can be such crippling guilt, disabling anger and a pain that shatters the heart and soul of one who loves them unconditionally. The anger towards a loved one can be a heavy cross to shoulder. Guilt can drive the anger that now fills the heart of one who has been bereaved.

We can also feel extremely angry with God. This can be particularly true for a person who has always had a strong connection with God. There can be a sense of anger with God for standing idly by and doing absolutely nothing to help our loved one during a time of illness. If God had intervened then my loved one would not have died. Such a feeling recalls Martha's statement to Jesus about her brother Lazarus: If you had been here my brother would not have died (John 11:21). There can be such strong anger with God for his non-intervention, for his failure to do something, some little thing to save the one we now long to hold again. All the things that have been left unsaid, all the plans that now remain unfulfilled permeate the heart and anger radiates from the knowing that it is now too late. Anger is directed at a God who stood by and let our loved one slip away from us. One can be especially angry with God in the wake of a death by suicide. There are now so many questions that will remain unanswered forever. There is the awareness that the pain of one we loved went unspoken and unheard. We can feel angry with a God who didn't heal the pain of one we loved so much. There can be anger with a God who allowed our loved one to die in an accident. This can be such a sudden and cruel way to lose someone and the hurt and the anger can be so raw, to disabling. For the parent who has perhaps waited many years to become pregnant only to have their hopes dashed cruelly through miscarriage or stillbirth, the anger with God can be so strong. The pain of a parent forced to leave a hospital with empty arms is heart-breaking and the anger expressed to a God who allowed this to happen is gut-wrenching. To stand along-side a broken hearted parent is to inhabit an abyss of nothingness. The cry that comes from deep within is akin to the cry of Jesus as he gave up his life on the cross (Matthew 27:46). It is raw. It is cutting. It is darkness and desolation at its worst.

There can also be anger with God as there is a sense that prayers have been left unanswered. When we know that our loved one is ill, we turn our attention to God and we beg him to turn his ear towards our plea. However, many times despite our pleading and our entreating, our loved one still leaves us. We are angry with God for abandoning us in our time of need. Despite all our attempts to live a good life, to do the right thing, to be the best person that we can be, our prayers have gone unanswered. No reward has been given for all that we have tried to do in our lives. We can feel like Job who felt that all his good work had been in vain, when he asked the Lord why is it that the good suffer while the wicked prosper? (Job 21:7). How come there has been no reward for services rendered to my God?

In many ways, we can feel punished. We can be furious with God because he has punished us for some past wrong-doing. Again, like Job, we can feel that this tragedy that has befallen us is some sort of punishment. Often while sitting with a person whose heart is breaking, questions around the will of God or the hand of God can be asked and it seems empty to simply say that God's ways are not our ways, but the reality is there are no answers, no formula to make it all better.

Anger is a primary emotion and behind the anger there is always another feeling. Anger with God often masks disappointment. We are disappointed and hurt that he has not saved us from this hell of pain, from this abyss of darkness or from this roadway of agony. We are engulfed in a world that seems endless. There seems to be the feeling that this will be my world for infinity and my God did nothing to shield me from it.

When we are angry we ought to allow ourselves to really feel the feeling. When we are angry with God, with ourselves and with the world we need to express it. Suppression of such a strong emotion can be so destructive. When we feel such intense anger we do

ourselves justice by expressing it. We may need to cry or to shout and this is perfectly justifiable. The best thing we can do at this stage in our journey is to be real – real with ourselves, real with our families, real with our friends, real with our world and real with our God. Be angry, be disappointed with God and tell him how you feel. As adults we form a relationship with him that is mature and is based on mutuality. Speak to him as you would anyone else. Express your anger to him. Tell him of your pain and your hurt. Ask him to touch the heart within you that is broken. Ask him to touch each beat of your heart, which exudes pain, brokenness and sorrow.

Where is God in all of this?

In the Garden of Gethsemane, Jesus Christ begged and pleaded with his father to remove the cup of suffering from him. He prayed not to have to walk the pathway that had been allotted to him. Simultaneously however, he accepted that it would be the will of the Father and not his own which would be done, so he handed his fate over to God. Where is God when we entreat him to take our cup of suffering away? Where does he stand when we fall on our knees and implore him to stop the torture within? Where is God when our world is consumed by darkness and desolation? Where is God when all we can embrace is nothingness? God is by our side. He extends his hand to the broken hearted and he places it within ours and he walks with us. God carries us when we do not have the strength to continue walking the roadway of life ourselves. God holds us and loves us when we stare into the darkness. He wipes away the tears from our cheeks when our hearts and souls heave in pain.

What am I to do?

The Bereaved

Anger can be very difficult to feel or to experience. If you feel anger, express it. Allow your anger to come to the surface and sit with it. Do not try to push it away or suppress. If you do, this anger will become destructive. It will harness more and more anger and eventually will turn itself into bitterness. Bitterness corrodes our inner goodness, so try not to embrace this particular emotion.

The Companion on the Journey

It is not easy to sit with the anger of others. But try to be a compassionate and supportive presence to your friend or loved one who simply needs you to be present. All they want from you is your love, your understanding and your willingness to sit with their pain. By giving of your time and love to another human being you are giving them the best gift ever. It is a gift finer than any gold or silver.

Bargaining:
brokering a deal to make the pain go away

Bargaining is considered to be the third stage of grief. A somewhat natural reaction to pain, helplessness, brokenness or vulnerability is to become gripped with a need to regain control. This can mean control over self, over our emotions, over others, over our lives or indeed over the pain and hurt that we have been feeling. 'If' is such a small word and yet it has such big connotations. 'If only' are words which permeate the bargaining period of the grieving process. If only this was not real; if only my loved one could come back to me; if only this was just a bad dream; if only I had not said what I did; if only I had tried harder to help; if only I had paid more attention; if only I had shown them more love; if only this was not happening to me.

When we lose someone we love our hearts feel pain like never before. At this point, the anger that once permeated our hearts and souls has abated and we are really beginning to feel the feeling underneath the anger. Our situation is now so very real. We have become so aware of the gravity of our loss. There is no hiding from the pain. Neither is there anywhere to run from the pain of our loss, from the pain of our guilt, from the pain of our regret, or from the pain of our new reality. The heart has been cut open and the pain is seeping through. Our bodies are aching like never before.

At this stage we feel so vulnerable. We have been cruelly disempowered. We have started to feel as if we have lost control of our emotions and of our bodies. We are at a loss as to how we can make the thumping pain stop. There can be an overwhelming desire to run from the pain but we find that there really is nowhere to go.

'If only' kicks in and we start looking for ways to navigate away from our pain and our sadness. We begin to see that negotiating a compromise with God might just happen to be the way out of this abyss. It just might provide a means of escape from the pain deep within. If we do a deal with God, if we bargain with him to make the pain go away, then things might just get better.

When we try to bargain, or to do a deal with God we are trying to run from the pain of our life as it is right now. If only a deal can be made with God. If this were to happen we would become shielded from the harsh reality of the here and now. Protection from the pain of my world would then surely be mine?

This stage of grief is a time of desperation and desolation. The pain of our loss has become so heavy to shoulder. The cross that we carry in our hands has filled us with fear and dread, a hopelessness that we fear we will never be able to shift. As we stare into the abyss of nothingness, the road that leads to darkness, we would do anything to make the pain go away.

As we begin to bargain to make the pain leave us, we become master negotiators. We have ideas around what we can offer to God if only he would shield us from our pain. We offer him the promise of a reformed lifestyle. We swear that if our pain goes away, that if our hearts become renewed and filled with strength to carry on, that we will give up all our vices and will forever do the right thing. We can offer time abroad volunteering, money for the poor, the giving up of old habits, or simply to be the type of person we have always struggled to be. In our desperation there is within us a need to promise anything that will take away our pain and that will ease our sadness and our loss. We need to regain control of who we are and we will promise anything to make this happen. These are sad and lonely days. There is such a longing to get back to normal and such a burning desire to walk back into life as it once was. In order to make this happen, bargaining is all that is left. The roadway has become so painful to travel that we will promise anything so that we have the strength to begin anew, to walk with gusto once more.

WHERE IS GOD IN ALL OF THIS?

God is the focal point of this stage of grief. God is the one we turn to in order to broker a deal. He is the one who will wipe away the tears from our cheek. He is the one who has the power to make things new again. God is targeted perhaps like never before. We beg him to answer our prayers. We entreat him to open his ear to the voice of our pleading. We knock on the door and we hope in desperation that he will hear the prayers that are spoken and unspoken at this time. We hope and pray that he will shine a light into the crevices of a broken heart and a heaving soul. We ask that God carry us along as we try to rebuild a life that has been so cruelly pulled apart.

God enters the world of the broken-hearted and he gives them the strength and the courage to carry on. God holds us in the palm of his hand and gives us the voice to ask for help. God gently lets us know that he is there at our back willing us to keep going. There are no loud noises, no great displays of affection, but He is there in the silence.

As Elijah heard the voice of the Lord in the gentle breeze, those who bargain with God come to hear his voice in the silence of their desperation.

What am I to do?

The Bereaved

Remain true to your emotions at this stage. Feel the desperation and the hopelessness and the anger within. Be honest with those around you that you are desperate for your pain to go away. Try to break open your heart and soul to God. He is suffering the pain of your loss so that as you suffer, he suffers too. Clothe yourself with compassion, kindness, humility, gentleness and patience. (Colossians 3:12)

THE COMPANION ON THE JOURNEY

If someone you care about is mourning, touch them with your love. They are desperate for the pain to go away. They are also hungry for your support and your understanding. Gift them your time and patience, love and compassion. Be a friend to someone whose heart is broken. Take their hand in yours and walk the roadway of pain with them.

Depression: Feeling the sadness of my heart

The fourth stage of grief is filled with a deep sadness. There is no denying the gravity of the situation now. The anger has abated and the bargaining has ended. All that is left in its place is a hurt that no words or actions can heal. The reality is that our loved one is not coming back. There will never again be a moment when we will speak to them, nor hear their voice or shake in laughter with them. As we recall our loved one, memories come flooding back. We remember the good times shared together. There were so many events that we shared that we now recall fondly but sadly. We reflect on so many things that happened between us and we are filled with the awareness that all we are left with now are our memories.

We now know that we are facing a future devoid of their presence, their love and their support. We miss their companionship, their listening ear, their supportive presence and the gift of their love.

Our sadness can take many forms. We can become filled once more with regrets. We are sorry about the words we should have spoken but didn't; the support we could have given and perhaps feel we didn't; we regret time spent apart from them thanks to the busyness of our life; we feel a sorrow for not appreciating the gift of their love and friendship while they were with us; we just want them back to tell them that we love them. But we know this is not possible. We know that we are now separated from them forever.

Parallel to our regret are our worries. Not only are we missing the person we love, but our minds can become full of practical, everyday concerns at this stage. We begin to worry how we will cope on so many different levels in this new and painful reality that is now our life. We long for the physical presence of our loved one but we are dealing not just with their loss and the many other emotions their death has aroused within us, but we are also wondering how we will cope financially.

The death of a spouse can have huge ramifications on the financial stability of a household so not only can one be grieving a huge loss, but are now perhaps also worrying about how to cope financially. Pinned to the pain of loneliness is the array of other financial, emotional and physical consequences of the loss of a beloved one.

At this stage, people speak of struggling physically and emotionally as a result of the myriad of issues they are now faced with. Sleep can be disturbed. Night after night there can be endless hours of broken sleep. No rest comes to a weary body as the mind is racing, packed full of thoughts and fears and worries about the pain of the present reality and the uncertainty of the future. Sleep recharges the batteries and without it a person becomes deeper engrained into a world of sadness and loneliness.

The appetite is also often affected during these days. Food no longer can appeal to one who previously had loved their food. There is nothing that can please the appetite that has been so cruelly quenched. Or perhaps the opposite can also happen, where a person finds comfort in food. Food can provide a momentary solace from the physical and emotional upheaval within. Fatigue and lack of energy also hits those who are grieving. Even when sleep comes it is not restful sleep so the body remains exhausted, spun out and weary. Energy has been spent on trying to get through the hell of each day so there is nothing left in the tank to keep moving. People speak of such overwhelming tiredness during these difficult days. The mind, body and soul are weary. There is no energy, no inclination at all to live life. The burden of sadness is so very heavy.

These are extremely difficult days both physically and emotionally. The tiredness affects not just the body but the emotions too. We can feel so lonely, so isolated and so alone. We feel a pain in our hearts that nothing can quench and nothing can heal. There is a feeling that no one knows our pain or understands the experience of our loss. We feel empty. Our hearts are broken and our souls have been decimated. Our loss makes us different. We are anxious and we stand alone in a world that does not seem to know us anymore.

We can feel guilt around our feelings and around our experiences. We can feel full of self-pity and we can cry loudly and from the soul during these days and weeks. Crying spells are very common at this juncture. These are hard and painful days. When we feel depressed we feel affected in mind, body and soul.

These are the times when perhaps we could seek out a bereavement counsellor or a chaplain who we can talk to about our feelings. To have a listening ear from outside our family and our immediate circle of friends can be particularly helpful at this juncture. When we feel alone and misunderstood it can be helpful to have someone from the outside to listen to us, to really hear what we are saying and to journey with us. It is a gift to have someone who will not judge us or belittle us and simply let us be. An intimate stranger can be there to hold our pain with us and help us to try to make sense of it all. The chaplain or counsellor will extend the hand of hope to you when it is needed. Simply to have someone to be there for you can be of huge benefit to help you see that you can carry on, that you have the power deep within, despite the great sadness, to walk on. There is a companion out there who can help you to begin to find hope and meaning once more.

WHERE IS GOD IN ALL OF THIS?

These are sad and desolate days. God at this point is weeping with you. Remember how Jesus wept at the grave of his friend Lazarus? His heart was broken and his soul was crying out in pain at the loss of his friend. God the Father held him in his pain. A powerful image of loss is Michelangelo's Pieta, where Mary holds the dead body of her beloved son in her arms. Imagine the pain Mary must have felt after carrying that baby within her womb at the request of God the Father for nine months, and given birth in a stable in Bethlehem, only to watch him die on a wooden cross on Calvary. How desolate her days must have been in the aftermath of his crucifixion? How alone she must have felt in her grief? Where did she get the strength to carry on? How did she manage to remove the image of her son on a cross from her mind? The hand of God touched hers and somehow she found the power and the strength within to carry on despite the pain of her grief, the weight of her loss and the brutality of her experience.

What am I to do?

The Bereaved

These are sad and difficult days. These are the hours that seem endless. The pain and the loneliness can seem unceasing. However, turn to your God and place your pain at the foot of the Cross. Tell the suffering servant foretold by Isaiah in chapter 53 that you need him to help you carry your pain. Tell those who you trust that you feel sad, lost and alone.

Offer the hand of hope to those who struggle with loneliness and desolation during these days. Offer no false hope or do not walk away from their pain of loss. Difficult as it is to see someone down, sad and feeling alone, allow them to feel as they do and try to encourage them to express their pain to someone they can trust. Just be there for the person you love who is finding it all so very difficult to shoulder the yoke of bereavement.

Acceptance: having the courage to walk forward with trepidation and hope

After the death of Jesus on the Cross, came his Resurrection into new life. There comes a point in the grieving process when one feels a little stronger in themselves. They begin to feel capable of beginning anew. They feel that they are ready to walk slowly, tentatively and humbly along their new pathway. There is the awareness deep within that although still sad and hurt and at a loss around the death of a loved one, there is now a gradual acceptance of what is now the reality of my life. Having gained the strength to journey through the pain of the loss, the hurt, the anger and the guilt – there is now a deepening sense that inner strength is beginning to grow. There is a tentative hope that life, although changed forever, can be embraced once more. There has come a little courage that ensures that a grieving person is strong enough to begin to re-adjust to the world as it is, without the person who once formed such a central tenet of it. There has probably begun a need to re-define one's role and place within the world. The death of a loved one can erode a person's sense of role. How does one feel when they are no longer a husband or a wife but rather are now a widow or widower? How does one feel when they are no longer a parent, a sibling, a carer, or a friend? The new reality needs space for the expression, exploration and the living out of such fears and emotions. In the acceptance stage, there can be energy, ability and scope to look at role definition or perhaps re-definition. There may now be brevity to begin to see anew the possibilities that now lay ahead. It can be the period when one becomes able to re-invest in other people and in other activities. There can emerge the ability to gradually let go of the heavy pain and burden of grief. In accepting the changed reality of life, in feeling strong enough to walk the new pathway of my life, comes not a forgetting of the loved one or of an experience, but rather a sense that now I can miss but let them go. I can remember with love and sadness but also with courage and strength.

WHERE IS GOD IN ALL OF THIS?

These are the days where the hope of the resurrection begins to enter our world. Having journeyed through the pain and desolation of our loss we begin to embrace not the suffering Jesus but the healing Jesus and the Risen Jesus. The pain, the sadness, the anger, the guilt and the burden of our loss has started to slowly move from our shoulders. The God who extended the hand of support to his heart-broken son Jesus in the Garden of Gethsemane has done likewise to those who have moved into the realm of acceptance. The God who wiped away the tears of Mary, the mother of his son, has also begun to dry the tears of those who mourn. God offers the healing touch of a Father who cares for the broken-hearted, the desolate and the lonely. Blessed are those who mourn, for they shall be comforted (Matthew 5:4).

What am I to do?

The Bereaved

For those who have started to embrace a life changed but full of possibility, walk slowly. Stand tall with hope in your heart but walk the pathway of change at the pace that best suits you. Do each and every day what helps you to reach out and embrace the life that now is yours. Do not feel forced into doing anything you are not comfortable with. Remain true to the feelings within and if you still stumble from time to time do not allow yourself to be filled with guilt or regret. Life is a learning process and it takes courage and determination to move into a world that is strange and challenging to you. Walk slowly and ask for help and support when you need it. Rely on family and friends who have the ability to walk with the 'new' you. Reach out and touch the world of hope that is now yours remembering that the love you have shared with another human being has made you the person you now are. Remember that you carry within you their love, their loss, their experience and their support for the future. You walk with God and your loved one by your side.

The Companion on the Journey

During these days of renewed strength and hope, your bereaved relative or friend needs you to share in their courage to begin walking the pathway of new life. Be a rock of support at this exciting and yet apprehensive time for them. Although seized with a new sense of hope and purpose, there are still many emotions that can raise their heads in these days. Be gentle, be present, and be supportively encouraging by affirming the new hope and the new possibility that is now theirs. They need a friend who will guide them compassionately and without judgment in the days ahead.

Conclusion

To endure a loss of any kind is heart-breaking, and as each of us is different, so too do we vary in how we react to the ups and downs of life. No matter what shape our life takes, the reality is that we will all be faced with a significant loss at some stage or another. How we will react is impossible to predict.

In reality, none of us know what it is like to endure the deep pain of loss and grief until we are forced into that particular abyss of desolation. It really is true that in order to extend the hand of empathy, we need to walk in the shoes of those who suffer. It is only when our hearts are shattered into millions of tiny pieces that we come to feel that intense pain of desolation and of loss. It is only when our souls heave in pain that we touch into the hopelessness of the suffering Jesus.

But as we journey through our loss, we encounter many glimpses of hope. We experience the smile of a friend, the outstretched hand of a virtual stranger telling us that they feel our pain, the offer of a walk, a drive or a lunch when really all we want to do is to remain within the cocoon of pain that is ours. In the goodness of others who long to reach us in our time of need we experience the love, empathy and compassion of a God who holds each of us in the palm of his hand. In the abyss of darkness comes the hope that we can begin anew, that we can and will smile once more.

We become strong enough to miss the person we loved and to let them go, not forgetting but remembering with love and hope.

WHAT FOLLOWS HERE ARE A SELECTION OF

Prayers and Readings

THAT MAY OFFER SOME SUPPORT DURING TIMES OF PAIN AND DESOLATION

Psalm 17: 1-2:

Listen, Yahweh, to an
    upright cause,
Pay attention to my cry,
Lend an ear to my prayer,
My lips free from deceit
From your presence will
    issue my vindication
Your eyes fixed on what is
    right.

Psalm 17: 8

Guard me as the pupil of
    an eye,
Shelter me in the shadow
    of your wings.

Psalm 18: 2

God is my rock and my
    fortress
My deliverer is my God
I take refuge in him, my
    rock,
My shield, my saving
    strength
My stronghold, my
    place of refuge.

Psalm 18: 6

I cried to God in my
    anguish
I cried for help to my God
From his Temple he heard
    my voice,
My cry came to his ears.

Psalm 23:

The Lord is my Shepherd,
    there is nothing I shall
    want.
Fresh and green are the
    pastures where he gives
    me repose.
Near restful waters he
    leads me to revive my
    drooping spirit
He guides me along the
    right path, he is true to
    his name.
If I were to walk in the
    valley of darkness, no
    evil would I fear
For you are there, with
    your crook and with your

staff and with these you give me comfort.

Psalm 90: 1-2, 16-17

Lord you have been our refuge
From one generation to the next.
Before the mountains were born,
Before the earth and the world came to birth,
From eternity to eternity you are God.
Show your servants the deeds you do,
Let their children enjoy your splendour
May the sweetness of the Lord be upon us,
To confirm the work we have done.

Ecclesiastes 3-8

There is a season for everything, a time for every occupation under heaven:
A time for giving birth,
A time for dying;
A time for planting,
A time for uprooting what has been planted.

A time for killing,
A time for healing;
A time for knocking down,
A time for building.
A time for tears,
A time for laughter;
A time for mourning,
A time for dancing.
A time for throwing stones away,
A time for gathering them;
A time for embracing,
A time to refrain from embracing.
A time for searching,
A time for losing;
A time for keeping,
A time for discarding.
A time for tearing,
A time for sewing;
A time for keeping silent,
A time for speaking.
A time for loving,
A time for hating;
A time for war,
A time for peace.

Jeremiah 4-5

Before I formed you in the womb I knew you; before you came to birth I consecrated you.

Matthew 4:4

Man does not live on bread alone, but on every word that comes from the mouth of God.

Matthew 5: 3-10

How blessed are the poor in spirit:
The kingdom of heaven is theirs.
Blessed are the gentle:
They shall have the earth as their inheritance.
Blessed are those who mourn:
They shall be comforted.
Blessed are those who hunger and thirst for righteousness:
They shall have their fill.
Blessed are the merciful:
They shall have mercy shown them.
Blessed are the pure in heart:
They shall see God.
Blessed are the peacemakers:
They shall be recognised as children of God.
Blessed are those who are persecuted in the cause of right:
The kingdom of heaven is theirs.

Matthew 6: 5-6

And when you pray, do not imitate the hypocrites: they love to say their prayers standing up in the synagogues and at the street corners for people to see them. In truth I tell you, they have had their reward. But when you pray, go to your private room, shut yourself in, and so pray to your father who is in that secret place, and your Father who sees all that is done in secret will reward you.

Luke 4: 18-19

The Spirit of the Lord is on me, for he has anointed me to bring good news to the afflicted. He has sent me to proclaim liberty to captives, sight to the blind, to let the oppressed go free, to proclaim a year of favour from the Lord.

THE FOLLOWING MAY ALSO BE USED AS INTERCESSORY PRAYERS DURING MASS OR A LITURGY BY ADDING *LORD HEAR US OR LORD HEAR OUR PRAYER* AT THE END OF EACH OF THEM:

The ministry of Jesus was full of healing miracles and Jesus Christ who came not to be served but to serve went about doing good and healing those who were in need of healing. Loving Father during these moments of great personal sorrow we ask for the gift of healing for those who are in need of it for whatever reason.

Jesus Christ gave sight to the blind and he raised up the lowly. He cured the sick and sought out the broken-hearted. We remember in a special way those who struggle in mind, body or soul and we ask that they and their families may receive the healing touch of God.

The prophet Jeremiah assures us that before He formed us in the womb God knew us. Tonight we pray that we may always have the courage to open our hearts to our Creator God and to trust in his plan for us and for our lives.

Each of us may not experience a miracle as such in our lives, but we do experience the healing touch of God in so many ways. We do so in the smile of another, in a kind word, in a supportive presence, in a listening ear. In the love of another human being, we find the love and support of both the suffering and the healing Jesus. For this, we give you thanks loving Father.

We remember all who struggle in mind, body or soul. We ask Lord that they will find love and support from a community who can reach out and touch their brokenness and pain.

As a community of believers we pray for those who are finding it difficult to believe in a loving and caring God. We ask that they may know the presence of God in their lives, the companion God who travelled the Road to Emmaus with his lonely and down-hearted disciples.

The prophet Jeremiah tells us that God knew us even before we were formed in the womb. We pray that we will always have the courage and the strength to bring our pain, our sadness and our vulnerability to the God who knows us better than we know ourselves.

We pray for those who are struggling with their faith. We ask that those who cannot see you in the darkness of their lives may come to see the light of the Risen Christ.

We remember those who are weighed down by the burdens of life. We ask you Lord that you may remove the rock of suffering from their hearts and let them feel the warmth of your love carrying them and supporting them.

Loving father during these moments of pain and desolation we ask you to carry us in the palm of your hand. We long to feel the warmth of your loving embrace and we pray that we may experience the healing touch that only you alone can offer.

God our Father as we sit at the foot of the Cross of your Son, we place the burdens of our heart and soul at your feet. We beg you to reach out and touch the brokenness, which we now carry deep within us. Heal us with your love and compassion.

We ask for the courage and the strength to continue to journey through the pain and the darkness of our life. Shine the light of hope and support into the brokenness of our souls.

46